# I Was There Too

# I Was There Too

*A Collection of Poems and Illustrations*

REESE M WILLIS

Illustrated by LISA OZVOLDIK

To request permissions, contact the publisher at reesewillis2013@gmail.com

Cover art and illustrations by Lisa Ozvoldik

ISBN 978-0-578-98750-7

# Author's Note

I began writing this collection of poems in the fall of 2018. Some of the poems were written back then, and some were written several weeks before publication. Consequently, their themes and styles vary.

If there is one thing that connects all these poems, it is the pure outward and optimistic idea that even in the darkest of times life is beautiful.

For Lisa

Your heart carries a nostalgic innocence for dreams yet to come
– a beauty that I will always try to capture.

# Contents

## in her heart

in her heart

she never grew
i still see her there
the beauty that never flew

in her heart

she laughs everyday
for there is beauty
beyond anything i can say

in her heart

she is youthful
seventeen years old again
but time can be so brutal

in her heart

i still see her
despite time's decay
her love will never blur

in her heart
she plays
games and dances
and spills pizza on my shirt

in her heart

all rhythm
breaks the pattern
of time

in her heart

we still go on adventures
we fight about driving
and that one time i lost the keys

in her heart

she is the autumn leaves
the winter silence
the cicadas in the summer
and every bit of spring

in her heart

she is
the girl i always loved
and time and eternity are but
two words

in her heart

we still wonder:

"what are we going to be when we grow up?"

a dream we never thought we'd reach
and everything was infinite

in her heart

## you are art

your life is a sculpture that can never be found

create yourself

for you are greater than david
and more serene than rodin's courtesan

with pain, and love, and hatred
continue the sculpture of your life

with your blunt chisel
and
hypercritical hammer

with muscle and bone and heart
dedicated upon marble
and flesh

you will get
cracked and smudged and chipped

but you are art
but you are art

and all the colors of a starry night
are but half whispers in front of
what van gogh truly saw:

you are but art
with every perfect flaw

and stripped of perfection
you are perfect

you will cry and bleed and sweat
upon the painting of your story

but you are art
but you are art

## until we fall asleep

when the world scars your heart
i'll sing you a song
and though it may be bad
and the key wrong

you'll smile
and laugh
and love the world again

and when the weight of that world
take its toll on me
you'll be there
to part the sea
with hugs
and kisses
until i fall asleep

but when

(and not if)

one of us sleeps
the world away forever
with a body stiff

and cold
and hollowed away
with time we carried together

there we will always be the notion

which carries a happiness
so beautifully profound
and deeper than the ocean

we had the present
and i'll always hold the past

(or you will hold mine)

and i think my dear
that will be just fine

i will have loved you

(and you will have loved me)

because even if we were vampires
the world still has to end
and would love be love
or a kiss transcend?

(i think not)

so we'll smile
and laugh
and love the world
with hugs and kiss

until we fall asleep

## somewhere beyond the moon

you must be somewhere beyond the moon
where the stars fiddle
and the planets dance

where the seas of the milky way
hold beautiful mysteries just for you

don't feel sorry for me
when you left i knew
you'd be free

somewhere beyond the moon
where pain is gone
and stardust colors your cheeks

where cancer is your constellation
and comets have no final destination

don't feel sorry for me
i have my telescope
so i'll always be able to see

beyond the moon
where i know you'll wait for me

## above and below the stars

in an insignificant place
with an insignificant breeze
we stared into the endless night sky

i was below the stars

drowning in insignificance
i felt emptier than
what contains them

fading gases

(silent
indifferent
and alone)

ephemeral only to god

all the tears of love and suffering
are but the imperceptible
vibrations of a half atom
waning in existence

below the stars

you were above the stars
you saw their perfect fire

(which illuminates your perfect existence)

laughing you touched my arm
look how they flicker
and shine

you said

how magnificently
they remain among the nebulae
locked in eternity's waltz

god's magnum opus
you spoke
with only them and us and infinity

smiling
i looked into your unraveled soul
and saw your meaning

i could hear the music

of a significant breeze
in a significant place

above and below the stars

with only them and us and infinity

## life is a daydream

life is a daydream
and i love there are stars
behind the yellow moon
melted like wax
          dripping with moonbeams

life is a daydream
reminiscent of your canvas body
resting on spears of grass
twirling in the summer wind
          in a summer painting

and the oceans who
endlessly cradle this wind
with each crashing wave
of their genius hands
          tells me everything

everything beautiful
everything ineffable
from the silent shadow of dusk
to the blazing dawn
          of dreams in your eyes

so i fight the wonderful fight
on the precipice of dreams
a step before the doorway of eternity
i inhale life before me
and life is a daydream

# beyond the aspens

maybe you'll find yourself
vacant
in a café off 70
with a broken heart

a vacant wallet
and a dream vacant of you

perhaps you'll find yourself
wholly in love
with wholly infinite stars
above our campfire

that will burn with you
in the future still
beating your heart
below the morning mountains

maybe you'll find yourself
stranded
the car won't start
and what about the future?

where and who and what
will you be?

perhaps you'll find
yourself

somewhere and
somehow
beyond the aspens
and before an ocean
with dreams more true

truer than me
truer than you

maybe it's best to focus

the future on a career
so you can live
a comfortable life
and sleep

on a comfortable bed
in a comfortable home

don't think of now
when you could think of later
because tomorrow must be certain?

but perhaps
you'll find yourself
in my arms
or any arms you choose

living a dream
of the western sun
or an eastern moon

basking in the ocean of the present
under fiery stars
that would burn
with you still

but maybe
you'll find yourself
home and seventy
the future secured and comfortable

dreaming of our campfire
and the ocean beyond the aspens
that could have been

truer than me
truer than you

but remain a wholly vacant dream

## two-way mirrors

directionless she wandered the empty space
far from the booms of the ordinary
and the burden of purpose

she wasn't supposed to be there
nobody was

supposed to
breathe success and pose
for two-way mirrors

'look at my perfect body'
'look at my perfect worth'

beyond the cold lens
and the impossible standards

all are inferior

because the highlight reels
broke her thumbs
and killed her soul

and so she stood before the fall
and the wind carried her thoughts

better than any medium could

and society's saddest story

repeats
and repeats

## in my cube

indifferent
unfulfilled passions and grace

dreaming days that won't come
we line the entrance
of the rat race

my cube is
beige and divested of spirit
i wear my poker face

it tightens around me
and dispossesses my art

from my cube
i can see them
cutting down plath's fig tree

i'm comfortable
i'm snug
but i don't want to be

i want to cry
but most of the time i can't
and when i do
i don't know why

i'm only twenty-six
holding the last figs in my hands

thinking of the bright white buzzing lights
and work politics

every morning i see sisyphus
happy to roll his rock

he didn't even have to challenge the
gods
he just sets his alarm clock

the numbers are sanguine red

# the wind that carries

today i listened to the flies
and
sometimes death is gentler than life

so
i thought of you
and that hunting knife
you gave me by surprise

i hope i still have it

somewhere

i hope i still have something from you
because
forgotten gifts renew

my fading memories
and become more significant

than time passed away
i was half america away

listening to the birds
when i heard you left

and
sometimes life seems infinite
if
you can believe that

so
now i listen to the ether

because
life is just ethereal

and death
like the kansas rain

or
the wind that carries your ashes

## nature's rarest blue

she was a blue bird

and she sang of a waxing moon
the silver sight
and a perfect spring night

she was nature's rarest blue
and freer than god himself

but
i caged that blue fire bird
in my vanity
my vanity so large so vast
and so hollow

for a time she loved me
and i thought i loved her too
but she was natures rarest blue
and her spirit was on fire

i tried to hold her fire
and keep it warm
but she lost her hue

she sung of the deepest blue
and it echoed softly
in the crater of my heart
like a morning dove
cooing above the dew

and it whispered there
a weeping so beautiful
that sometimes i wept too

so in our deepest winter
i set her free
to a waning moon
and a silent wind

my cage was all but shrunk
and she kissed the door
the whispers became a scream
for a moment

but upon her flight
she sustained god's colors

and all echoes ceased to exist
and all echoes ceased to exist

like a forgotten dream

## your ageless heart

perhaps time kills our hearts
and children grow old
and beer bottles
spill and stain

where toys used to
imagine great worlds
like neverland
which sadly never was

perhaps dreams become practical
and safe
the mysteries not so mysterious
and the inquisitive heart loses its glow

our bones become tired
on the weekends
our minds like a static radio

but i know that will not be
your heart is ageless
it dances and sings
and you with it

it's ethereal
like a crisp morning mist
and the breeze that holds
the autumn leaves

while they dance suspended
and sing softly to the ground

i know you will carry that spirit
and capture it for me

your drawings hold
that childhood dream

and they feel like the moon
over a meadow
or the music of the ocean
falling to the shore

time may age your mind
but your spirt will draw

and dance
and love
and sing

fully and wholly
which forever carries
your ageless heart

## the dreams we lived

if your stubborn wanderlust
were less than the size of the rain

or the nostalgic moon
beckoned for a tired place
somewhere i've never been

i would tempt the gods of spring
and sing orpheus a song

if your weary heart
was quieter to me than the proud stars

or the winds of tomorrow
carried your essence
beyond my grasp

i would resplendently dream of you
and yesterday's gentle breeze

if your heavenly presence
found itself other arms

i would think of every blessed smile
you still have to give

because the heaven you give me
is true and endless

because forgetting is like stealing a star
from a world that never existed

i will always carry the dreams we lived

and all the beautiful moments change
like the planets dancing around the sun

or young flowers blooming
before dawn

## plastic memories

buy some more followers
take a picture everywhere you go
fake important friends make you glow
and stand out

look at yourself travel the small world
make another mirror
you'll stop seeing yourself if you bring it nearer
without a doubt

you cradle your ego
in someone else's hands
don't let it slip
they could be your fans
and don't think about

memories genuine and true
that no lens captured
or ever could recapture

edit them out

with plastic memories
worth a thousand plastic thumbs
and a thousand empty hearts

## her perfect ambivalence

i could dance upon her flaming moon
like a dreamer above dawn

i could fall into
her cold twilight
and drown in the perfect silence
in the sapphire waves of her eyes

ever changing
and breathless

i would excavate the silver
lining her clouds
boundless for her amber sky
and a future full of everywhere

and no matter the matter
of where i discover her
i would follow her maze
and stay lost

my heart would follow

her perfect ambivalence

## season 67

watch another episode
see how the series ends
and don't think about stolen time

watch another episode
and come in early
so you have some show time

watch another episode
and forget
"what value do you bring?"

watch another episode
when you're sick
because it comes out of two weeks

watch another episode
because you only have two days
to not think about the other five

watch another episode
and pretend to be busy
so you can survive

maybe one day
you'll be sixty-seven
with nothing but time

and hopefully not
already in heaven
with wings made of dollars

and stolen time

## you stood before an ocean

you felt the midwest rain
the air crisping cold
and the thunder wrapped around your heart
you let the
warm rain fall
through you

i saw you on the threshold
you almost touched
the gods

then

you stood before an ocean
the salty water tickling your feet
and the clouds danced through the breeze
that lifted your hope

all facades fell short
in that moment

then

you embraced the silent snow
the blood in your cheeks
looked warmer than cocoa
you were so
beautifully significant

but you didn't notice
the ecstasy of a moment
over and over again
(sorrowfully)

but my dear

you are
the matter
the material
the substance

of nature's grand soul

every second you touched the rain
and made the angels jealous

i saw your essence
and the meaning of a moment

## the bloated boy

we were immigrants on the shore
floating on may
sunflowers and maze alike

shining resplendent
between infinite spaces of
manifested destiny and buffalo

then a railroad a pump or two
dress the land with our success
rivers slept under films

then the smog of success
followed with its poison weightlessness
drying the tears along the trail

now our towers of fake gold
only shined fake hope

“give me your tired”
“give me your poor”
we lied

a beacon for the immigrants
all bloated on the shore

only trying to escape war

they were immigrants on the shore

the bloated boy
"yearning to breathe free"

floating on the water
he saw a golden door

"give me your tired"
"give me your poor"

## a cocktail of hate

anger i drink you
and you taste more
addicting every tip of the chin
the clank of the bottles
implore another

anger i drink
and like the sharp dioxide
that rivers my throat
the same familiar sting
is felt nationwide
and then nullified

my land is a pandemic on fire

fear i drink you
straight and sharp
you greet me most nights
but sometimes i greet you

fear i drink
because i know
it's you i'll never outgrow
like a secret tumor

and all things are out of my control

grief i drink you
you're new and hard to get down

like cold absinthe
i try to regurgitate you
but you stay put

grief i drink
because those we lost
are so much more than just pronouns
or political arguments in a hometown

so my body takes another drink
my mind thinks of humanity

a cocktail of hate

and my spirit apologizes

## my blue heart

bare and naked on the grass
she left her heart
soaking in the morning dew
clear as glass

the blood fell
and ran through
like autumn leaves
trickling towards the cold cold ground

she walked away
and did not turn
for she knew

i could not share
the heart inside of me
caged and blue and scared
to be free

her heart was still beating
pure and whole and red
but as she faded away
its rhythm stopped dancing

and now it sits there
on the cold cold ground

silent and still
empty of everything

it used to see in me

only the autumn wind
and the stained leaves
leave a sound

they painted my memory

with every smile
and every laugh
and every inexplicable moment of beauty

and everything my cold little heart
was scared to embrace
was left for me

she left it all for me
on the cold cold ground

where the autumn leaves danced
in the silent wind

## ivory towers

we were happily lost

somewhere in paris
and maybe prague

like a bee crossing the ocean for a flower
unsure of what came next
we built an ivory tower

and we stayed lost
in budapest
and barcelona

like children hiding
from each other

we did not address the issue
that one day i would leave
and miss you

one last trip to venice
and in vienna we said goodbye

as our tower faltered

somewhere in america
i returned alone
and altered

from eight to five
i dreamt of you

and our ivory tower
and all of its beautiful pieces

but you crossed the ocean
and i stole you

like hades and persephone

and now you're here
and the summer wind holds us still
while we wait for winter

with all the beautiful pieces

## a place like a garden

i thought heaven was
a place
like
a garden

with tomatoes and lavender
and a symphony of birds
and bugs
with nowhere else to be

no

now i think

it's a road
and your feet are on the dash
you're shaping the clouds
asking if i can see

your animal in the sky

and the road goes
and goes
goes

it's so hauntingly real
the essence is like a song

no
now i think

it’s your heavenly whisper
which holds the moon
like the breeze
under a soft spring night

we’re on a porch

the bugs transpose
our song

in the distance
there is a garden
with tomatoes and lavender
but all splendors and symphonies

fade into the silent nocturnal
the echo barely reaching the road

your eyes
your soul
your presence
is perfect

and heaven is there

## old man eating breakfast alone in a restaurant

old man whom do you go home to?
is there anyone waiting for you
or just a faded memory
of something you once possessed?

old man were you once a champion
young and wild and ready to take on the world
or were you quiet and happy and content
waiting for the world's treasures to find you?

tell me who you are now old man.
does she wait for you
or are waiting for her?
has there ever been a her?
what private moments that took your breath away
and gave you life

i hope you had those.

old man do you keep those memories that you carried
or did you leave them behind in times
purposefully forgotten?

do i really understand the nostalgia of a moment?

old man i am scared.
does time hurt more than loss?
will i be the same man i once was?
will they see that?

old man who are you now?

sitting in your silent reserve
alone or ignored?
have you been forgotten
or left behind?

as the hand winds
are you speeding it up
or trying to slow it down?

old man i'm scared.
i'm scared of a future remembering the past
of being stuck under the memories of youth
drowning in the waves of the present.

old man who were you back then?

## dreaming birds

i was worse and worrisome
for this unkind world

for what majesty wasn't smudged?
what beauty wasn't judged?
and what heart never broken?

i was hoping for hope
and a sign of serenity

but man kills and thrills
and defeats the world
and the world defeats
everything perfect and beautiful

so i hid in my cabin
outside of man
veiled of the world
and dreamt of birds

peaceful and blue

and one hushed night
i heard words
of one dreamt bird

i threw the door

and hoped
to my core

but i saw an owl
abreast
          feathery
                    and proud
upon the winded tree

i marveled
she did not call
but only bowed
in the whispering wind

a bluebird whimpering in her talons

# grandparents

when he sat alone there
and how the peppered light
collapsed on your empty chair

the calm silence
like the dreamless sea
was everywhere

you each had your hugs to give
and so he sat there
with only one to receive
from the young boy that was me

who was too scared for goodbye
when you dreamlessly pulled your anchor
for the dreamless sea

and though he sat there alone
while you silently sailed the gentle water
to a place perhaps

with birch trees
behind the giant horizon
he knew you were finally at ease

and so a brief moment ago
he gave his last hug
and left his chair

and though sometimes
we may sit alone
in life's unfair harbor

he knew one day
he must set sail
for the horizon beyond dreams

and to a place perhaps
with birch trees
and warm hugs

## borrowed dreams

sometimes i don't feel

like a real person

sometimes i think
the dreams i achieved
were only yours

borrowed from the others
and theirs borrowed too

now we live our borrowed dreams
and though i have
flesh and thoughts

ears to hear the music

i can only feel the tempo increase

and most times
i forget there was
ever any music at all

but the tempo still surges

like a broken drum
beaten by a broken robot

so i march
every day

to this broken beat

i wish it would slow down
i wish i could make my own music

but borrowed dreams are easier

than hunger
than hope

than humanity

sometimes i dream
the music i could make

if the robot would
ever break

but the drum keeps
beating

and beating
and beating

## perhaps for a moment

perhaps you will stop
and see the clouds for what they are
accidentally lighthearted on a hilltop

perhaps for a moment you will exist
tracing daydreams along the clouds

with your celestial eyes
confronting the celestial sky
finally forgetting the future
and singing goodbye

to the pervasive past
like the perfectly present flowers
who betray their not-so-secret truth
who forget the meaning of hours

perhaps you will see it there
the moment for what it is
with accidental flowers in your hair

perhaps for a moment you will simply exist
tracing daydreams along the clouds

with the perfectly present flowers

## tonight when it snows

tonight when it snows
we won't hear a thing
except perhaps
          a naive fire
                    or a shriek
the hot cocoa on my clothes

tonight when it snows
when we forget the sorrowful wind
and learn to love the stains
          of the life we chose
                    we'll burn the fig leaves
and never look away

tonight when it snows
we'll forget yesterday
and just enjoy the innocent silence
          of the improbable snow
                    leaping softly from the silent sky

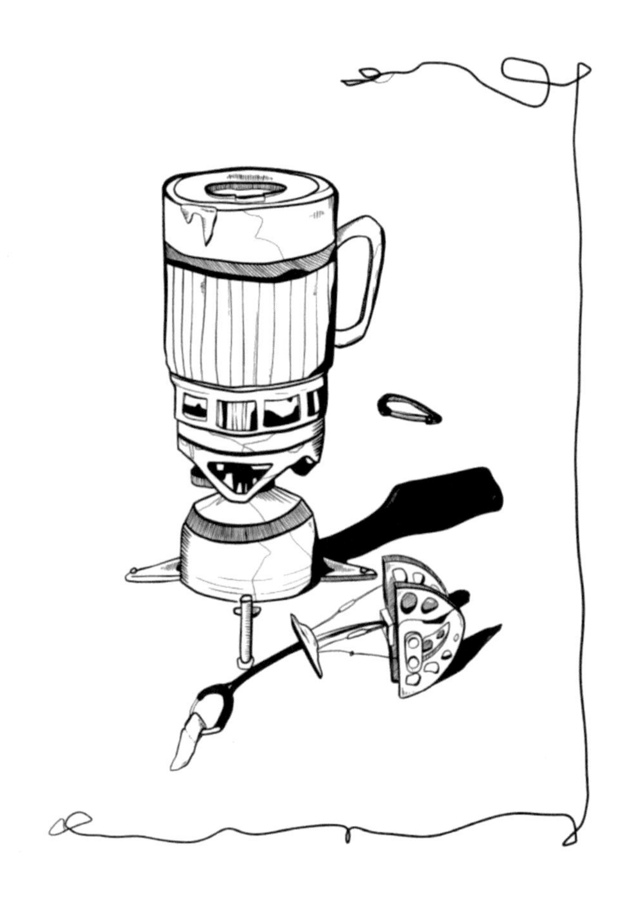

## the freedom i would never have

before the boundless white
and a precipice overlooking
a winter creek

i took in the sight
and here the wind whispered stories
          from time immemorial

(your fire burns here

hear your existence
where only the creaks
of boreal groves
force their opinions

and judgment is left
before the mountains

lose the droves that carry on
the sick routine

so weeks can fade
into weeks
and money into comfort)

the creek below echoed the wind

(hear your fire burn

the crackle and spark

of life under the pines

there is no time
to waste when existence
is simply existed)

and the infinite beauty
of the stars silent
          trees rooting
                    the primordial mountains
curved by the rivers of infinite time

and all things sacred
and majestic

untouched by routine
          and hollow men

          silently shouted to me

and so i saw
          as it were

a small fire in the distance
perhaps a cabin in the woods

and above
          a single hawk bounding
                    towards the boundless horizon

she carried my thoughts
(and all the freedom I would never have)

and all things sacred
and majestic

## artist on the beach

i wish i was a poet
and i wish you were an artist

i wish we were drinking wine
and napping in french meadows

i wish we didn't work in boxes
without purpose and formal clothes

and think about mondays
or what happens next in the series

i wish we were always chasing each other
somewhere on a beach

where the full moon is our spotlight
and the adriatic our audience

(something more than just a figure of speech)

i wish we didn't have to plan anything
or only express the convenient emotions

because we can't ruin the weekend
so we have to go through the motions

i wish i could express in words
that no matter where

or how
or when

this imperfect setting we find ourselves in
you are perfect beyond measure

i love you

and that will always be tried and true

you're an artist painting my heart
like the moonlight painting the beach

so for now that will make do

## sleeping bears

if we could be bears
and if the rain could illuminate
perhaps the language
of the honest trees
or the scared stars

(which timidly dance and sing
the honest meaning of things)

if we could be bears
just waking up
to the rhythm of the mountains

our paws so large
cusping life
and drinking its free frosty water

if we could be bears
and our titan ears
would hear a true hush

if we could just be bears
and if it was sometimes true

where all our cares
rush down the fluent current

of humanity's river

then perhaps for a moment
the gods will wake us

from our young sleep

## snowbird

you gave me a rose
          a rose from jericho

you packed your clothes

(and the sun
          and the moon
fell on other shores)

for this land that is
so far and so broken

i was there too

your heart descended to me
and i embraced you
like an albatross around your neck

far from the snows
who descend perfectly
over the city of music

and the voice of your mysterious heart
(sometimes your parted soul)

breathed beautifully
like the salt inside the sea

but you are a snowbird

and this so far and so broken land
broke your wings

and that mysterious voice

(like the snow)
became fragile and crestfallen

it gestured for home

the sound of your eyes
          the melody of your body

compelled me carefully

feather by feather
to pluck the albatross

          so here i fill steinbeck's box

          (poem by poem; verse by verse
          my invincible love for you)

i promised
a rose from jericho

while we wait

(for the sun and the moon
          to fall on other shores)

we’ll perfectly dream

of the musical city
and the snow that descends
beautifully everywhere

for you are a snowbird
    who innocently chases the music

    for dreams yet to come

# About the Author

Born and raised in Augusta, Kansas, Reese went on to The University of Kansas where he kindled his love for poetry, literature, and rock climbing (but double majored in Chemistry & Biochemistry for some reason). While at university he met his wife and illustrator Lisa. The pair currently reside in Reno, Nevada where they further pursue their love for poetry, literature, the outdoors, and each other.

# About the Illustrator

Lisa was born and raised in Vienna, Austria where she developed her passion for art and snowboarding. During university she decided to study abroad; however, she never thought she would end up in Kansas where she would meet Reese (she originally wanted to study in Canada). Lisa now resides in Reno, Nevada with Reese where she continues shredding the American powder and occasionally drawing beautiful pictures.

Made in the USA
Middletown, DE
20 November 2022